TIME TRAVEL GUIDES

THE AZTEC EMPIRE

Jane Bingham

Raintree

Chicago, Illinois

© 2007 Raintree
Published by Raintree,
A division of Reed Elsevier Inc.
Chicago, Illinois

Customer Service 888-363-4266

Visit our website at www.heinemannraintree.com

Designed by Steve Mead and Geoff Ward
Photo research by Erica Newbery
Illustrations by Eikon Illustration & Tim Slade.
Printed by South China Printing Company Limited

11 10 09 08
10 9 8 7 6 5 4 3 2

Library of Congress Cataloging-in-Publication Data
Bingham, Jane.
   The Aztec empire / Jane Bingham.
      p. cm. – (Time travel guides)
   Includes bibliographical references and index.
   ISBN-13: 978-1-4109-2730-9 (lib. bdg.)
   ISBN-10: 1-4109-2730-X (lib. bdg.)
   ISBN-13: 978-1-4109-2737-8 (pbk.)
   ISBN-10: 1-4109-2737-7 (pbk.)
1. Aztecs–Guidebooks–Juvenile literature. 2. Mexico
City
(Mexico)–Guidebooks–Juvenile literature. I. Title.
   F1219.73.B56 2007
   972'.01–dc22
                              2006033875

Acknowledgments
The publishers would like to thank the following for
permission to reproduce photographs:
AKG Images **pp. 13**, **14**, **27**, **48**; Alamy **pp. 36** (Nature
Picture Library), **41** (Visual Arts Library), **43** (World
Pictures Ltd.), **46** (Gary Cook); Art Archive **pp 8**, **24-25**,
27, **38-39**, **44-45** (2007 Banco de Mexico Diego Rivera
& Frida Kahlo Museums Trust. Av. Cinco de Mayo No. 2,
Col. Centro, Del. Cuauhtemoc 06059, Mexico, D.F.), **26**
(Museo Ciudad, Mexico/Dagli Orti), **32-33**, **39**, **50-51**,
53 (Museo del Templo Mayor, Mexico/Dagli Orti),
49 (Museum für Völkerkunde, Vienna/Dagli Orti), **21**
(National Anthropological Museum, Mexico City/Dagli
Orti), **8**, **37**, **38-39**, **44-45** (National Palace, Mexico
City/Dagli Orti), **22**, **35** (Templo Mayor Library, Mexico/
Dagli Orti), **29** (Dagli Orti), **54-55** (Nicolas Sapieha),
16, **18**, **19**, **21**, **30**, **47**, **52**; Bridgeman **pp. 56-57**; Corbis
p. 31 (Macduff Everton); Digital Vision **p. 10**; Getty
Images **pp. 12** (The Image Bank/Gabriel M Covian), **6-7**
(National Geographic/Stephen Alvarez); NHPA **p. 30**
(Kevin Schafer); Scala Archives/British Museum, London
p. 23.

Cover photograph of an Aztec pyramid reproduced with
permission of Alamy Images/Hugh Taylor. Photograph
of the Stone of the Sun reproduced with permission of
Ancient Art & Architecture Collection Ltd/ Dr.S.Coyne.
Photograph of an ornament in the form of a double-
headed serpent reproduced with permission of the
Werner Forman Archive/British Museum, London.

The publishers would like to thank Paul Steele for his
assistance in the preparation of this book.

Every effort has been made to contact copyright holders
of any material reproduced in this book. Any omissions
will be rectified in subsequent printings if notice is given
to the publishers.

Disclaimer
All the Internet addresses (URLs) given in this book were
valid at the time of going to press. However, due to the
dynamic nature of the Internet, some addresses may
have changed, or sites may have changed or ceased to
exist since publication. While the author and publishers
regret any inconvenience this may cause readers, no
responsibility for any such changes can be accepted by
either the author or the publishers

CONTENTS

Map of the Aztec Empire 4

Facts About the Aztec Empire 7

City on a Lake 25

Travel, Food, and Shelter 33

Things to See and Do 39

Going Shopping 45

Health and Safety 51

Aztec Empire Facts and Figures 55

Further Reading 61

Glossary 62

Index 64

Words that appear in the text in bold, **like this**, are explained in the Glossary.

WVALLEY OF MEXICO

GULF OF MEXICO

N
W E
S

Tuxpan

Tula

Teotihuacán

Lake
Texcoco

Tenochtitlán

TENOCHTITLÁN

TWIN VOLCANOES
POPOCATÉPETL &
IXTACÍHUATL

Huaxyacac

PACIFIC OCEAN

Mexico

Gulf of
Mexico

Pacific Ocean

Central
America

South
America

AZTEC EMPIRE

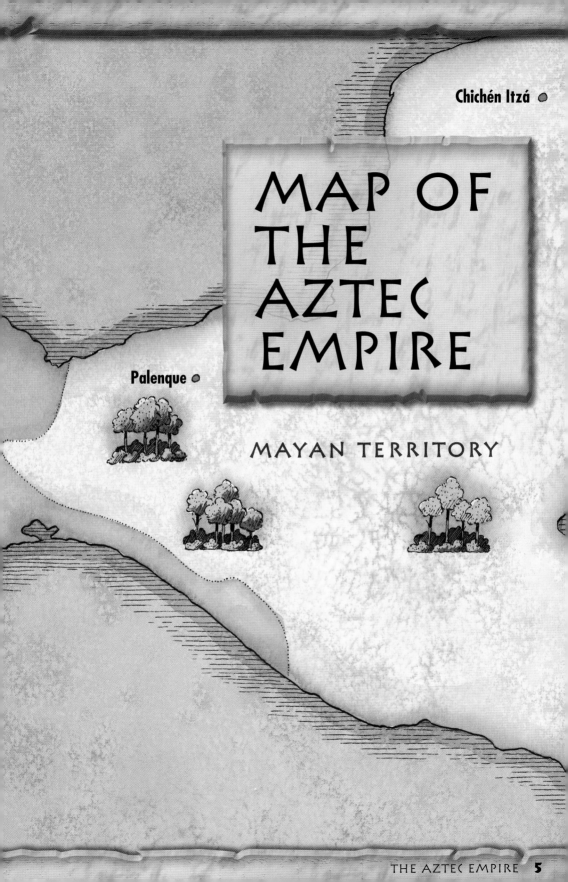

Chichén Itzá •

MAP OF THE AZTEC EMPIRE

MAYAN TERRITORY

Palenque •

A river trip through the spectacular scenery of the rainforests is a must when visiting the Aztec Empire.

CHAPTER 1

FACTS ABOUT THE AZTEC EMPIRE

If you're a fan of vacations with a dash of danger, the Aztec Empire is just the place for you. You can trek through steamy rainforests, climb towering mountains, and see some amazing wildlife. But the highlight of your trip must be a visit to Tenochtitlán, the city on a lake. Here, you can tour stunning buildings and witness colorful (and bloodthirsty!) ceremonies. There are also great opportunities for shopping and eating out.

A trip to the Aztec Empire is not for the squeamish, and you may even find yourself fighting for your life. But armed with this guide and a bit of luck, you will have a vacation you'll never forget!

WHEN TO TRAVEL

The Aztec civilization began around 1150 CE and lasted until 1521, when it was taken over by Spanish invaders. This means you have less than 400 years in which to visit the Aztecs.

If you arrive in Mexico in 1325, the Aztecs will have settled on the shores of Lake Texcoco, where they will be busy constructing their city of Tenochtitlán from a series of islands in the lake.

BUILDING AN EMPIRE

Visitors to Lake Texcoco around 1440 will be amazed by the sight of the city of Tenochtitlán, linked to the **mainland** by gleaming stone **causeways**. In the 15th century the Aztecs worked hard to build up their empire. Aztec warriors fought rival tribes to gain more territory, farmers **cultivated** the land, and **merchants** traded with their newly conquered people. During the early years of the empire, you will be able to watch the rise of a great civilization.

To see the Aztec Empire at its best, plan to visit around 1510. You will find an empire of some six million people, ruled by a powerful emperor with a mighty army. There are thriving villages, towns, and **city-states**.

This modern painting shows how the capital city of Tenochtitlán may have looked in the 1500s. It was then at its largest and most spectacular.

Locusts often attacked the Aztecs' maize crops. Look carefully and you'll see some in this picture.

TIMES TO AVOID

Whenever you plan your trip, watch out for **plague**, **famine**, and flood. Don't visit the empire in 1446 or 1507 when pests overrun Tenochtitlán and farmers' harvests are ruined.

After 1519 you should stay away from the Aztec Empire. Hernán Cortés arrives at this time with his Spanish army, determined to conquer the Aztecs. Within two years, Cortés has destroyed most of the Aztecs' finest buildings and sent many of their treasures back to Spain. By 1521 you'll find the mighty Aztec Empire in ruins. You'll also be in danger of catching **smallpox**. The Spanish brought this deadly disease to Mexico. It spread rapidly among the Aztec people.

GOOD AND BAD TIMES

1325 CE	The Aztecs settle on the shores of Lake Texcoco
1400s	The Aztecs begin to build up their empire
1446	Plague of **locusts**
1450–1454	Famine
1490–1500	The Aztec Empire is very powerful
1500	Floods in Tenochtitlán
1505	Famine
1507	Earthquake and plague of rats
1508–1518	The Aztec Empire is at its largest
1519	Spanish troops arrive
1520	Smallpox spreads through the empire
1521	The Aztec Empire is destroyed

Key:

	Stay away
	Okay times to visit
	Best times to visit

GEOGRAPHY AND CLIMATE

The Aztec Empire stretches from the Gulf of Mexico to the Pacific Ocean. It measures about 108,000 square miles (280,000 square kilometers). Compared with other ancient empires, the Aztec Empire isn't vast. But it covers an amazing range of different landscapes.

FROM COAST TO PEAKS

Along the empire's coasts there are sandy beaches and stretches of rock. You'll come across a few small fishing villages, but don't expect much action. There are very few towns along the coast.

Farther inland, the land flattens out as you reach the coastal **plains**. Enjoy the sight of the farmers working in their fields, but remember to watch your step. This flat, **fertile** region can be very swampy.

At the center of the Aztec Empire is a large area of tropical rainforest.

At the heart of the Aztec Empire is a spectacular area of tropical rainforests, rugged mountains, fast-flowing rivers, and large, tranquil lakes. This is where most of the cities are found. The central mountainous heart of the Aztec lands is worth exploring, but be sure to take a local guide with you. The rainforests can be impossible to get through, and some towns and villages can be reached only by narrow and dangerous mountain passes.

WATCH THE WEATHER

Visitors to the Aztec Empire need to come prepared for all kinds of weather. In the plains and rainforests it is hot and steamy, but high up in the mountains the temperature can drop to well below freezing, especially at night.

If possible, try to avoid the rainy season, which lasts from June to October. At this time of year you will probably experience heavy rains and floods. However, the Aztecs also suffer from long periods of **drought**, when all their crops wither in the fields.

STORM ALERT!

If the weather gets stormy, you could be in trouble. The Aztecs believe that their god Tlaloc controls the rain, and they offer him gifts to keep him happy. These gifts include shells, models of frogs, and animal **sacrifices**. When the weather gets really bad, the Aztecs believe that Tlaloc is very angry. So they sacrifice children to him!

AGRICULTURE

In spite of the difficult weather, the Aztecs grow a wide range of produce. Farmers grow maize, beans, vegetables, fruit, and even flowers. All farming is done by hand using wooden tools. The Aztecs have no wheeled vehicles and no farm animals to help them.

Most farming takes place on the fertile coastal plains, but people in mountainous regions build **terraced** fields along the sides of the mountains. Some Aztec farmers grow their crops on floating fields in lakes. Look out for these floating fields, known as *chinampas*, in the waters of Lake Texcoco.

NATURAL RESOURCES

The Aztec Empire's many mountains are a rich source of **minerals**. The Aztecs mine for gold, silver, and copper as well as precious stones such as turquoise and jade. They also **quarry** their mountains for building stone and for a hard, volcanic rock called obsidian. These materials are used to make ornaments, weapons, and gifts for the gods. While you're in the market, look out for knives and arrowheads made from glassy obsidian, and for precious ornaments made from gold, silver, and turquoise.

ANGRY VOLCANOES

The twin volcanoes of Popocatépetl and Ixtacihuatl are a spectacular sight. But don't expect a guided tour of these peaks. The Aztecs believe these volcanoes are angry gods who are plotting to destroy the world.

WHO'S WHO IN THE AZTEC EMPIRE?

Before you head off to Mexico, it's a good idea to figure out exactly who does what in Aztec society. Aztecs are very status conscious. If you confuse an eagle knight with a serpent woman, you could end up in serious trouble!

AN ORGANIZED SOCIETY

Aztec society is very strictly organized, so people know exactly where they belong. At the top is the emperor, or *tlatoani*, who is treated like a god. He makes all the big decisions on when to go to war and how to govern his lands. Under him are the nobles who also perform the duties of priests. Next are the professional soldiers who spend their lives fighting other tribes. Below the soldiers are **commoners**. Some are free, but some have to work for masters. Commoners can be farmers, merchants, or craftworkers. Right at the bottom of Aztec society are the slaves. They can be bought and sold in the markets, and they often end their lives as human sacrifices.

MUTEZUMA

Rex ullimus Mexicanorum

Moctezuma II was the last Aztec emperor. He ruled from 1502 to 1520.

COUNCILS

Nobles have an important role to play in the Aztec Empire. They meet in councils to advise the emperor. The leading member of the council is known as the serpent woman, even though he's a man! The serpent woman, or *cihuaoatl*, is often the younger brother of the emperor.

CLANS

On a local level, Aztec society is divided into clans. These are large groups of up to 200 families. Each clan is run by a group of leaders who are responsible for the area's farms, markets, and schools.

All the male members of the clans have to perform some kind of service for the emperor. This may involve fighting in the army, helping build palaces or temples, or doing unpaid farming work. Craftworkers serve the emperor by making beautiful objects, such as carvings, masks, and headdresses. These objects may be worn by the emperor and his nobles or they may be presented to the gods.

An Aztec nobleman receives gifts from his workers.

CONQUERED TRIBES

Once the Aztec army has conquered a tribe, the lands and cities of that tribe become part of the empire. Each conquered tribe has to pay a form of tax to the emperor known as **tribute**. Tribute can include different kinds of cloth, animals and their skins, birds and their feathers, jade, maize, honey, rubber, and gold. The army also uses the prisoners they have captured as human sacrifices for their gods.

EAGLE KNIGHTS

Knights have a high status in Aztec society. Any man can become a knight, as long as he can fight bravely enough. If a commoner captures three enemies in battle and delivers them to a priest for sacrifice, he can be rewarded for his bravery by being made into an eagle knight. An eagle knight has the right to wear leather earplugs and an eagle-feathered headband. If you meet a man dressed like this, be careful not to upset him—you can be sure that he knows how to fight!

AZTEC CLOTHES

If you want to fit into Aztec society, you'll have to learn to dress like an Aztec. There are very strict rules, and commoners are not allowed to dress like nobles. Anyone who breaks the rules can be put to death.

Only the emperor and his nobles are allowed to wear clothes made from cotton. Everybody else has to dress in simple clothes made from maguey cloth. This is cloth woven from the threads of the maguey cactus. Nobles can wear sandals—except in the presence of the emperor—but commoners have to go barefoot. Nobles can also wear golden jewelry, but the commoners' jewelry is made from shells or polished stones.

CLOTHES FOR COMMONERS

All commoners wear the same basic style of dress. Men wear tunics knotted at the shoulder and reaching to their knees. Women have a loose top and a simple skirt. Usually these clothes are very plain, but sometimes they have colorful patterned borders.

High up in the mountains, people keep themselves warm by wearing a rectangular blanket knotted around their neck. These woven blankets are very useful. During the day they act as a cloak, and at night they are used as bedding.

In the warmer parts of the Aztec Empire, men wear simple loincloths, especially when they're working in the fields.

KEEPING CLEAN

The Aztecs are concerned with keeping clean. They wash their face regularly in cold water, and most families have a separate bathhouse outside their home. Aztec bathhouses work like modern-day saunas. The family lights a fire outside the bathhouse and waits until its mud walls are really hot. Then they go inside and throw water against the walls to produce steam. When the bathhouse is filled with steam, people beat their skin with bundles of sticks to make sure they get really clean.

NOBLE DRESS

Aztec nobles love to dress up in all their finery. Over their simple tunics they wear long cotton cloaks edged with precious jewels and embroidered with gold thread. Some cloaks are lined with rabbit fur, but the best cloaks are made from brightly colored feathers. Nobles also wear a lot of jewelry. As well as gold necklaces, armbands, and anklets, they wear lip, nose, and ear plugs made from gold and precious stones.

AZTEC CUSTOMS

You'd better make sure you do as you're told in the Aztec Empire. Everyone in the empire, from the nobles downward, is expected to work hard and to be obedient. Children learn at an early age to obey their parents. Anyone who dares to disobey has to face very harsh punishment.

LESSONS AT HOME

As soon as they are able to work, Aztec children are expected to help their parents. The children of farmers learn to work in the fields, while young craftworkers learn the secrets of their trade so they can help in their father's workshop. Boys are also taught general skills such as hunting, fishing, and handling a canoe.

CHILDREN BEWARE!

The picture below shows Aztec children being punished. Disobedient boys and girls are held over a fire made from chili peppers and forced to breathe in clouds of choking smoke. Sometimes naughty children have their skin pricked with cactus spines, and their hands and feet tied with ropes. Then they are left lying in a puddle for a day.

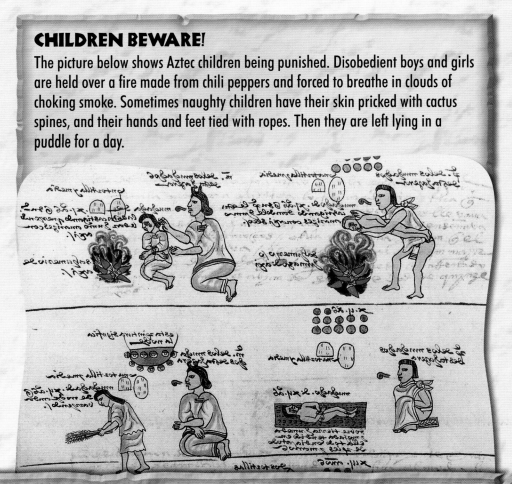

Girls learn how to run the home. By the time they are 12 years old, most Aztec girls know how to grind maize into corn and make bread. They also know how to spin thread and **weave** it into cloth.

AZTEC SCHOOLS

Most Aztec children go to a youth house, which is attached to the local temple. Here priests teach them about their history and religion. Boys learn building and fighting skills as well as weapon use. Girls learn how to be good wives and housekeepers.

The sons of noble families attend a special school where they are trained to be priests, members of the ruling council, or leaders of the army. They study history, religion, the art of war, and the science of astronomy.

TIME TO MARRY

Aztec girls are expected to marry around the age of 12 to 15 years old. Boys marry in their late teens. Marriages are usually arranged by the parents with the help of a wise man who acts as a matchmaker. Most Aztec men can only afford one wife, but nobles often have more. One Aztec noble was said to have had 200 wives and 144 children! Husbands are expected to protect their wives and earn enough money to support their families. Wives have to run the home and obey their husbands.

WORDS, NUMBERS, AND TIME

PICTURE WRITING

The Aztecs don't have an alphabet or numbers. But they do have a great way of writing things down. Instead of writing words, they use picture symbols known as **glyphs**. Often these glyphs show an object, a creature, or a person, but sometimes a glyph is a simple sign. For example, the Aztec sign for a journey is a set of footprints. The sign for war is a shield and arrows.

When the Aztecs want to show a number, they use dots—similar to the patterns on a set of dominoes. So the number seven is usually shown as a pattern of seven dots.

FOLDED BOOKS

Aztec books are made from long strips of bark or deer skin, folded up like a fan. The name given to this kind of book is a **codex**.

AZTEC CALENDARS

Aztec ideas about time are pretty complex. For a start, they use two different calendars! One calendar is used by priests to help them calculate when to hold festivals. The other calendar is used by normal citizens when they need to figure out important dates, such as market days.

In the everyday calendar, the year has 365 days (like our calendars today), but instead of 12 months there are 18. Each month has 20 days, which leaves five days at the end of the year. These five days are thought to be very unlucky.

The great
Stone of the Sun
(or Calendar Stone)
was kept on top of the Great Temple in
Tenochtitlán. The colorful pictographs
represent Aztec days, months, and years.

The two different calendars only come together every 52 years.
This is the time of the New Fire Ceremony. At this time, the Aztecs
believe that one major cycle of time comes to an end and another
begins (see page 40). The double time system used by the Aztecs
can be quite confusing. So if some Aztecs suggest a date to you,
remember to check which calendar they are using!

AZTEC RELIGION

In the Aztec Empire you'll come across **shrines** and temples devoted to the gods. The Aztecs believe that their gods control everything that happens in their lives. Each family has its own household gods. There are also gods for different crafts and times of the year. The Aztecs always try to keep their gods happy, although some of the things they do can be very gory!

AZTEC PRIESTS

As a sign of devotion to their gods, Aztec priests don't wash. They also pierce their flesh with cactus spikes. This means Aztec priests are easy to spot. They're the people with blackened clothes and faces, tangled hair, and torn and bleeding skin.

SACRIFICES TO THE GODS

The Aztecs believe that their gods can be kept happy by human sacrifices. Victims may be sacrificed by drowning, beheading, or by having their heart ripped out of their body. Then the victim's heart and blood are offered as gifts to the gods.

DON'T GET SACRIFICED!

Don't hang around too close to the Great Temple in Tenochtitlán. The Aztecs like to use foreigners for their nightly sacrifice to Huitzilopochtli. Usually, they use prisoners from enemy tribes, but don't take any chances.

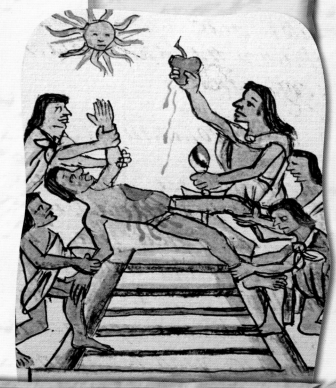

HUITZILOPOCHTLI

One of the most important Aztec gods is Huitzilopochtli. He is the special god of the Aztec rulers and the god of war. The chief shrine to Huitzilopochtli stands on top of the Great Temple in Tenochtitlán. Each evening at sundown, prisoners captured in battle are led up the temple steps to Huitzilopochtli's shrine. They are stretched on their back over a stone block while a priest cuts out their heart with a knife. The victims' hearts are burned as offerings to Huitzilopochtli, and the lifeless bodies are hurled down the steps.

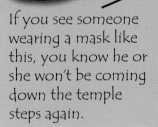

If you see someone wearing a mask like this, you know he or she won't be coming down the temple steps again.

ANIMAL GODS

Many Aztec gods are associated with wild creatures. Huitzilopochtli is sometimes known as the Hummingbird. Quetzalcoatl is known as the Feathered Serpent and is also associated with snakes and with the quetzal, a tropical bird.

GODS AND GODDESSES AT A GLANCE

- **Huitzilopochtli** — special god of the Aztec rulers; also associated with war and the sun.
- **Quetzalcoatl** — god of creation; also associated with rain and wind.
- **Tlaloc** — god of rain and lightning.
- **Xipe Totec** — god of vegetation and springtime.
- **Coatlicue** — goddess of the Earth.
- **Coyolxauhqui** — goddess of the moon.
- **Tonatiuh** — god of the sun.
- **Mictlantecuhtli** — god of death.

This modern painting of Tenochtitlán can be seen in the National Palace in Mexico City.

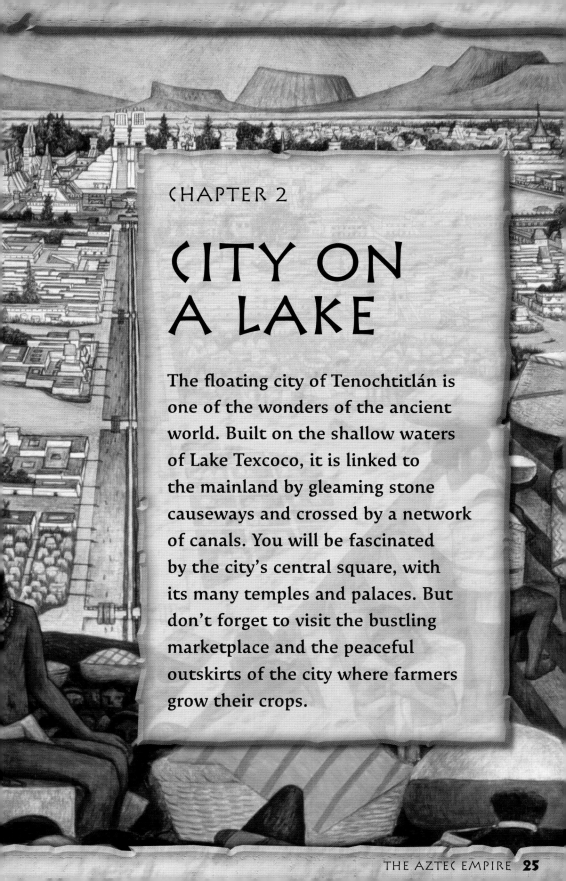

CHAPTER 2

CITY ON A LAKE

The floating city of Tenochtitlán is one of the wonders of the ancient world. Built on the shallow waters of Lake Texcoco, it is linked to the mainland by gleaming stone causeways and crossed by a network of canals. You will be fascinated by the city's central square, with its many temples and palaces. But don't forget to visit the bustling marketplace and the peaceful outskirts of the city where farmers grow their crops.

THE STORY OF TENOCHTITLÁN

In the 12th century, the Aztecs left their homeland in northern Mexico and traveled south in search of fertile lands. By 1250 they had reached the Valley of Mexico and, around 1325, they settled on the marshy shores of Lake Texcoco. Here the Aztecs began to construct a series of artificial islands, known as *chinampas*, made from water plants and mud, and held in place by walls of woven reeds. This was the start of the city of Tenochtitlán.

THE EAGLE AND THE CACTUS

The Aztecs have a legend that when their people first reached Lake Texcoco, they saw a white eagle perched on a cactus with a serpent grasped in its claws. The Aztecs recognized this as a sign from the gods that they should settle in this place. In Aztec picture writing, the eagle on the cactus is the sign for Tenochtitlán.

A GROWING CITY

At first, Tenochtitlán was simply a series of island farms linked by bridges. By the mid-14th century, it had become a well-organized city with a network of canals and roads. The city's early buildings were simple huts made from mud and reeds. Then, in the 1370s, Emperor Acamapichtli gave orders for the first stone buildings to be constructed. He also divided the city into four districts with a central **ceremonial** square at its heart.

BRILLIANT BUILDINGS

Emperor Moctezuma I built a giant pyramid to the god Huitzilopochtli in the central square of Tenochtitlán in the 1440s. He also built a royal palace surrounded by beautiful gardens. Later emperors followed Moctezuma's example, adding temples and palaces to the city center, and building stone causeways to link the city to the shore. Even the huge flood of 1500 wasn't allowed to wreck Tenochtitlán. Emperor Moctezuma II simply gave orders that his city should be completely rebuilt.

TWIN CITIES

Tenochtitlán is attached to a sister city, called Tlatelolco, which was built around the same time. Tlatelolco is the empire's busy commercial center. If you enjoy shopping, the markets of Tlatelolco are not to be missed.

THE END OF TENOCHTITLÁN

In 1519 Hernán Cortés and his Spanish troops arrived in Tenochtitlán and were stunned to see such a beautiful and well-organized city. Two years later they had conquered the Aztecs and taken charge of Tenochtitlán (see pages 56–57.) Cortés gave orders for the Aztec buildings to be flattened and a new city to be built. This was the end of Tenochtitlán and the start of the modern Mexico City.

This picture shows the Spanish arriving in southeastern Mexico in 1519.

EXPLORING TENOCHTITLÁN

At the heart of Tenochtitlán is the magnificent ceremonial square. This is where all the major religious ceremonies are held. This area is strictly out of bounds for commoners, so you'll need to wear your noble clothes. Plan to spend several days in this square, taking in the atmosphere and exploring the sights. But be warned—this experience is not for the faint-hearted!

THE GREAT TEMPLE

First stop on any tour must be the Great Temple, the tallest and grandest building in the empire. This magnificent pyramid measures 88 feet (27 meters) tall, with a steep flight of steps leading to its summit. But don't be tempted to climb these steps—you might become too closely involved in a human sacrifice!

Perched on top of the temple are two colorful shrines devoted to the worship of Tlaloc and Huitzilopochtli. The shrine to Tlaloc is colored blue, while Huitzilopochtli's shrine is painted red.

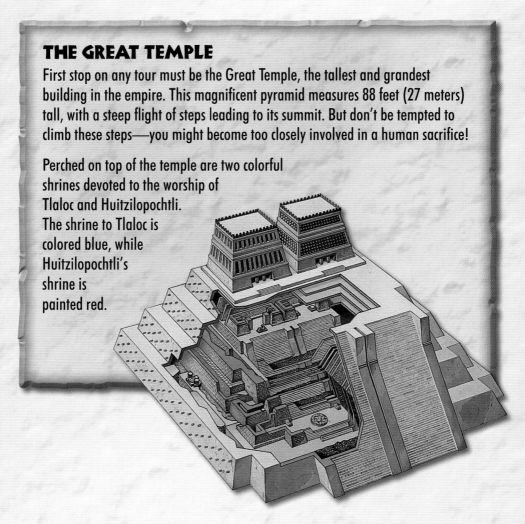

INSIDE THE GREAT TEMPLE

If you're very lucky, you might be allowed inside the Great Temple. This is where the Aztecs leave their offerings to the gods, and the temple is filled with carvings of gods and goddesses. There is also an amazing collection of precious gifts, including masks, necklaces, and ornaments made from gold, turquoise, and jade.

SKULL ALTAR

Close to the Great Temple is a large rectangular building known as the *tzompantli*, or skull rack. It is built entirely from the human skulls of sacrificial victims! Holes are drilled in the sides of the skulls so they can be displayed on poles. This photo shows a stone replica of the original skull rack.

Follow the maze of passageways past the remains of sacrificial victims. If you look around carefully, you will spot the skeletons of crocodiles and pumas, as well as the remains of jaguars, with green jade balls in their open mouths.

THE COYOLXAUHQUI STONE

Inside the Great Temple is a large, circular stone carved with the figure of the moon goddess Coyolxauhqui. According to Aztec legend, Coyolxauhqui fought a fierce battle with her brother, the sun god Huitzilopochtli, on a high mountaintop. Huitzilopochtli won the battle and killed his sister. Then he chopped up her body and threw it down the mountain. This is the origin of the Aztec custom of throwing the bodies of victims down the Great Temple steps after a human sacrifice.

MORE CITY SIGHTS

After the Great Temple, the biggest buildings in Tenochtitlán are the royal palaces. There are at least four palaces to explore, and they all have beautiful gardens with fountains and **reservoirs**. The palace of Emperor Moctezuma II even has its own private zoo!

MOCTEZUMA'S ZOO

The Emperor Moctezuma's zoo has a great collection of pumas, jaguars, and rattlesnakes. The zoo is especially famous for its birds. The emperor has 10 different bird pools in his gardens. Some provide homes for river birds, while others are filled with saltwater for seabirds.

The beautiful quetzal bird was considered sacred by the Aztecs. Its colorful feathers were used in the ceremonial dresses of emperors and priests.

ROYAL PALACES

Each palace is like a miniature town, with hundreds of different rooms and thousands of slaves to keep it running. As well as a grand throne room, guest rooms, and meeting halls, there are also countless libraries, storerooms, and workshops, and even dungeons for prisoners of war. Plan your visit to a royal palace when you have plenty of energy. An early Spanish visitor to Tenochtitlán reported that he had walked through a palace until his legs could carry him no further, and he still hadn't managed to see it all!

SACRED BALL COURT

While you're in the center of Tenochtitlán, don't forget to visit the sacred ball court. If you're lucky, you might see a game of *tlachtli* in action. This sacred game is played between two teams and is meant to symbolize the battle between life and death. *Tlachtli* is great spectator sport, but whatever you do, don't join in. The rumor is that the winning team is sacrificed to the gods!

ANCIENT GAME

Players of *tlachtli* wear leather helmets, arm and knee guards, and a padded leather belt. They try to hit a rubber ball using their arms, knees, and hips. Both teams aim to score points by shooting the ball through a stone hoop set high in the wall. The Aztecs didn't invent their sacred ball game. It was also played by the Maya (see page 43), who lived in Mexico before the Aztecs.

This picture from the Ciudad Museum in Mexico shows Aztecs marching toward the Valley of Mexico.

CHAPTER 3

TRAVEL, FOOD, AND SHELTER

Travel in the Aztec Empire is not for the faint-hearted. There are no wheeled vehicles and no animals to carry loads or people. This means you'll have to rely on your own two feet or travel by canoe. However, all the effort will be worth it. You'll see spectacular mountains, forests, swamps, and beaches, and stay in some interesting places along the way. You'll also enjoy some meals that should make your mouth (and your eyes) water!

ON THE MOVE

In most parts of the Aztec Empire, you'll have to travel by foot. To make matters worse, if you are traveling with commoners they will expect you to go barefoot. The only good news is that you might find a slave who will carry your luggage.

TRAVEL BY CANOE

Fortunately, the Aztec Empire has many lakes, rivers, and canals, so travel by canoe is easy. The Aztecs use flat-bottom canoes carved out of tree trunks. Handling these canoes is quite tricky, so try to find an Aztec to paddle you around. In Tenochtitlán there are hundreds of canals, and Lake Texcoco is a great place to fish. Try to persuade a local fisher to take you on a fishing expedition.

DON'T EVEN THINK OF FLYING!

Whatever you do, don't arrive in the Aztec Empire by plane. The Aztecs believe that their world will be destroyed by monsters from the sky.

Aztec townhouses usually have flat roofs with just a ground floor.

PLACES TO STAY

You won't find any guesthouses in the Aztec Empire, so if you want a place to stay you'll have to make friends with the local people. If you do get to stay in an Aztec home, you'll need to be very well behaved—and very lucky. The Aztecs' usual reaction to foreigners is to sacrifice them to their gods!

If you are fortunate, you might get to stay in the guest room of a royal palace, but you will probably have to settle for a family home. Aztec homes are made from mud bricks and have very few windows, so they can stay cool inside. They are very simply furnished, with reed mats on the floor and low benches and tables made from woven reeds.

In the country, houses have thatched roofs made from reeds. Aztec city houses usually have a flat roof and are just one **story** high. (Only nobles and emperors are allowed to build houses of two stories or more.) City houses are usually built in groups around a central courtyard, which is shared by several families.

⬆ These Aztec women are preparing a banquet.

If you stay with an Aztec family, you'll spend most of your time in the central courtyard. Most courtyards have a fire for cooking and a water pond. This is where the women work, preparing and cooking meals, and spinning and weaving clothes.

FOOD AND DRINK

Aztec food is hearty, wholesome, and filling. Most meals include a tortilla—a type of pancake made from maize flour—that can be wrapped around a range of fillings. The Aztecs have plenty of fresh ingredients, but you'll need to develop a taste for spicy foods. The Aztecs love chilis, and they put them in almost everything!

MOSTLY MAIZE

Maize is grown all over the Aztec Empire. It is the basic element of almost every meal. Sometimes it is eaten in the form of corn on the cob, but usually it is dried, ground into flour, and made into tortillas. Tortillas may be baked or steamed. They are usually served stuffed with beans and vegetables, but on special occasions meat or fish may be added to the filling.

VARIED VEGETABLES

If you like veggies, you are in for a treat. During your trip you will probably get the chance to eat peppers, tomatoes, leeks, squashes, watercress, and artichokes, to name just a few! The Aztecs also use onions, garlic, chilis, and different herbs to make their food taste more flavorful. Desserts are rare, but you may be served fresh plums or cherries with your meal.

MEAT, FISH, AND OTHER TREATS

Aztec farmers don't keep animals for their meat, but they do go fishing and hunting. This way, they manage to eat a wide range of dishes. As well as fish, duck, turkey, and deer, the Aztecs eat parrots, owls, eagles, lizards, and frogs. Birds' and insects' eggs are also considered a great treat.

VERY HOT CHOCOLATE

Aztec emperors like to end each day with a drink of hot chocolate. But it's not like the sweet chocolate drink you may have had. The emperor's drink is created from a mixture of **cacao beans**, vanilla, spices, and chili pods, which make it really hot and spicy!

If you are offered a chocolate drink, you should feel very honored. The Aztecs think that chocolate is the drink of the gods, and commoners are not allowed to try it.

CACTUS BEER
One of the Aztecs' favorite drinks is pulque, a type of beer made from the roots of a cactus plant.

The Aztecs used cacao beans as money as well as for making drinking chocolate. ➔

In this painting, the emperor (in blue feather headdress) is being offered gifts of fruit, tobacco, cacao, and vanilla.

CHAPTER 4

THINGS TO SEE AND DO

There's always something to do in the Aztec Empire. If you're a fan of music and dance, try joining in an Aztec festival. But be warned—they can be really wild! Or you may prefer to explore the beautiful countryside. Lurking in the Mexican rainforests are jaguars, pumas, toucans, parrots, and rattlesnakes, while the rivers are home to crocodiles, turtles, and many kinds of tropical fish. You can also learn about the ancestors of the Aztecs. Scattered all over the empire are the ruins of civilizations that helped shape the Aztec way of life.

CEREMONIES AND FESTIVALS

The Aztecs love putting on a show. But be careful to check what the celebration is about before going—sometimes it's best to stay away!

FREQUENT FESTIVALS

Each night in Tenochtitlán, priests make sacrifices to the sun (see page 23). There's also a major festival every 20 days, at the start of each new month (see page 20). Every spring, the ceremony to Xipe Totec, the god of spring, is performed. Farmers dance to encourage the corn to grow. If you look carefully at the dancers' cloaks, you'll see that they are made from the skins of the victims of human sacrifices. The cloaks are meant to symbolize the wrinkled leaves around the cobs of corn!

AZTEC WEDDINGS

Before a wedding ceremony, the bride's face is painted with yellow paint. Her arms and legs are covered in red feathers. Then she is carried in a torch-lit procession to the house of the bridegroom's parents. Here the couple sprinkles sweet-smelling **incense** over each other. Then the matchmaker (see page 19) knots the bridegroom's cloak to the bride's blouse as a sign that they are married.

NEW FIRE CEREMONY

The most dramatic ceremony of all is the new fire ceremony. It takes place every 52 years, so if you want to catch it you'll need to time your visit for the years 1403, 1455, or 1507.

The new fire ceremony marks a special time in the Aztec calendar, when a major cycle of years comes to an end and a new cycle begins. It begins with the binding of the years, in which 52 wooden rods are tied together to mark the end of the cycle. Then there is the lighting of the new fire for the start of the new cycle.

For 12 days before the new fire ceremony, people fear that the world will end. Houses are emptied of furniture, pots, and pans, and no one is allowed to light a fire. Everyone **fasts** on bread and water. At midnight on the 12th day, a fire is lit in the chest of a sacrificial victim. If the fire is lit correctly, then a new sun will rise in the morning, bringing about a new cycle of years. All the Aztec leaders gather in the ceremonial square in Tenochtitlán to wait for the sun to rise. When it does, everybody celebrates for days!

DEADLY FLOWERS!

The War of Flowers may sound pretty, but really it's a bloodbath. When the Aztecs are running low on sacrificial victims, two armies of knights battle against each other until their commanders decide that enough prisoners (sacrificial victims) have been taken. The battle takes its name from the colorful costumes of the knights. When the knights charge into battle, they look like a shower of falling blossoms!

ON THE HISTORY TRAIL

While you're in ancient Mexico, why not explore the history of this fascinating area? People began to settle in the Valley of Mexico as early as 9000 BCE. Between the years 300 BCE and the time of the Aztecs (around 1325 CE), several major civilizations flourished in the region. Each of these peoples built fine cities with stone temples, palaces, and statues to their gods. Their traditions were passed on from one civilization to the next, and were finally adopted by the Aztecs.

THE CITY OF TEOTIHUACÁN

Teotihuacán is the biggest ancient city in Central America. The Aztecs began building the city around 100 BCE. It gradually grew over the next four centuries. At the city's heart were two huge temples—the Pyramid of the Sun and the Pyramid of the Moon. They were linked by a grand avenue to a royal palace and a busy marketplace. Little is known about the people who built this impressive city, but it provided a model for many later civilizations.

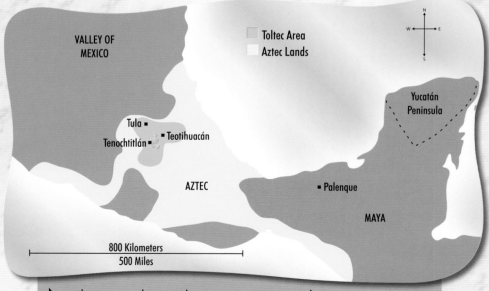

This map shows the major cities in the Aztec Empire.

MAYA

The Mayan civilization had its origins around 1500 BCE in the Yucatan peninsula, south of the area settled by the Aztecs. By around 250 CE, the Maya people were building cities out of stone in many parts of Mexico.

At Palenque, close to the eastern border of the Aztec lands, you can explore the remains of a great Mayan city, with temples, an **observatory**, and a ball court. The Maya were warlike people who took prisoners and sacrificed them to their gods. By the 1400s, when the Aztecs came to power, the great Mayan cities had been abandoned.

TOLTECS

The Toltecs were warriors, traders, and craftworkers who sacrificed prisoners to their gods. Around 1150 the Toltecs built a great city at Tula. If you visit this site, you will see giant stone warriors standing guard over the ruins. The Toltecs were eventually driven out of Mexico by neighboring tribes.

TOLTECS OR GODS?

By the time the Aztecs arrived in the Valley of Mexico, the Toltec city of Tula had been abandoned. The Aztecs dug among the ruins and took away many treasures. They were amazed by all the things the Toltecs had created, and believed that these people must have been powerful gods.

These giant statues of Toltec warriors can be seen in the ruins of Tula.

This modern painting shows a busy market day in Tenochtitlán.

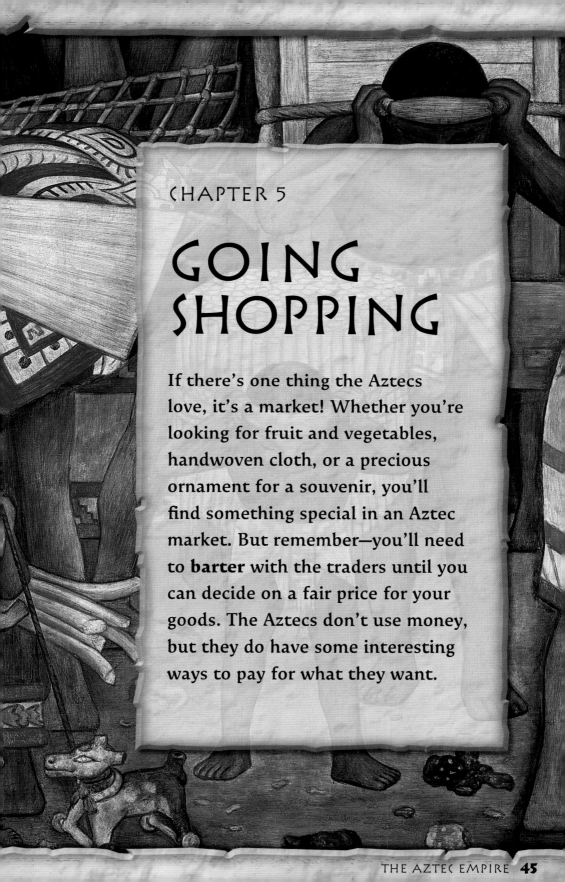

CHAPTER 5

GOING SHOPPING

If there's one thing the Aztecs love, it's a market! Whether you're looking for fruit and vegetables, handwoven cloth, or a precious ornament for a souvenir, you'll find something special in an Aztec market. But remember—you'll need to **barter** with the traders until you can decide on a fair price for your goods. The Aztecs don't use money, but they do have some interesting ways to pay for what they want.

AZTEC MARKETS

The best Aztec markets are in Tenochtitlán and its twin city of Tlatelolco. Every day is market day in Tenochtitlán, but a major market is held every fifth day. This is an occasion not to be missed, so remember to note it in your diary.

TENOCHTITLÁN MARKET

To get a flavor of the Tenochtitlán market, you'll need to be up at dawn. This is when you'll see the farmers arriving in their canoes. Watch them unloading boatloads of maize, fish, and vegetables, and setting up their stalls. By 8 a.m. you'll hardly be able to move in the large crowd, estimated to be more than 60,000 people!

Tenochtitlán market is divided into squares for the many different types of goods on sale. The market stretches over many miles, so you'll need at least a day to see most of it. High on your list of things to see must be the craft stalls (see pages 48–49), but don't miss out on all the other sights, sounds, and smells:

- Visit the grain traders' area and watch the farmers weighing piles of maize.
- See the timber stalls where carpenters are bargaining for logs, floated in from the rainforests.
- Drop in at the **masons'** area to buy stone, bricks, and tiles.

Feast your eyes on the colorful fruit, vegetables, and flowers straight from the rainforest.

Don't go home without a quick visit to the poultry section. There you'll be able to see (and hear!) pigeons, parrots, eagles, owls, and falcons, to name but a few. You can pick out a bird you like and then take it home, dead or alive!

WAYS TO PAY

Aztec traders accept gold grains, cacao beans, or copper bars as payment. Cacao beans and copper bars are useful as small change, but for larger purchases you'll need gold. Grains of gold are kept in goose **quills**, which come in different lengths. Traders will let you know what length of quill they want.

This picture shows traders with their wares at an Aztec market.

FAIR TRADING

Market prices aren't fixed, so be prepared to barter until you get the right price. But don't be afraid of getting tricked into a bad deal. Most big markets have a court of judges, who are there to deal with any problems. There are also officials who patrol the market, making sure that everyone is trading fairly.

HEAVEN CAN WAIT

"Given the choice between going to market and going to heaven, the normal Aztec housewife chose heaven, but asked if she could go to the market first!"
[A Spanish priest speaking around 1522.]

WHAT TO BUY

If you want to find some great souvenirs, head straight for the craft market. There you will see hundreds of stalls selling jewelry, carvings, pots, baskets, and clothes. You'll also have the chance to see Aztec craftworkers busy making their goods.

GOLD, TURQUOISE, AND FEATHERS

If money is not an issue, why not go for the most highly valued goods, made from gold, precious stones, and feathers? Aztec goldsmiths make a range of jewelry for the emperor and nobility, including breastplates, armbands, and ear plugs. These dramatic ornaments are often decorated with swirling patterns and **inlaid** with precious stones. Goldsmiths and stone carvers also create stunning masks and decorative swords, spears, and daggers.

Aztec masks are especially dramatic, with their glaring eyes and bared teeth. They are often made from seashells. Some masks are made from a highly polished volcanic stone called obsidian. Others are inlaid with hundreds of pieces of turquoise or jade.

If you want a really unusual gift, choose an example of Aztec featherwork. Feather workers use brightly colored feathers from tropical birds to make dramatic headdresses, cloaks, and shields. Woven into the feather designs are gold and jewels, to create a costume fit for an emperor.

MAKING A FEATHER SHIELD

Like most Aztec crafts, feather working is a family business. The women sort and dye the feathers, the children mix the glue from bat dung, and the men draw the shield design on a piece of cloth. Then the feathers are cut to shape and stuck onto the cloth. When the basic design is dry, the cloth is stretched over a board. More feathers are added, and the pattern is outlined in fine gold thread.

AZTEC POTTERY

For tourists with less cash to spare, pottery is a good option. At the expensive end of the market are decorated bowls used by nobles and priests, but you should also be able to find a good range of basic cooking pots. Other simple pottery objects are clay figures of the gods, vases for flowers, and pottery whistles used by Aztec dancers. You may even want to buy a small clay stamp. These are dipped in ink and used at festival time to print patterns on the dancers' faces.

This sacrificial knife was used by the Aztecs to cut out the hearts of their victims.

CHAPTER 6

HEALTH AND SAFETY

You need to be fit and strong—not to mention lucky—to survive in the Aztec Empire. Travelers to the empire may suffer from tropical fever or from exposure to the cold. They may be attacked by all kinds of wild creatures or by Aztec warriors. Plus, there's always the danger of becoming a human sacrifice.

HEALTH CARE

The Aztecs believe that diseases are sent by the gods as a punishment. However, there are several steps that you can take if you get sick.

AZTEC DOCTORS

If the market **remedies** don't help, try visiting an Aztec doctor (known as a *tlamatini*).

- For coughs and colds, a doctor may **prescribe** a steambath, a mint drink to relieve a congested chest, and a cough medicine made from honey or cactus juice.
- Patients with pimples may be treated with ointment and an herbal drink to purge their system.
- Doctors also know how to set broken bones using **splints**. They sew up wounds using hair.

However, not all the *tlamatini's* cures are reliable. If you have an earache, you may find a doctor pouring liquid rubber into your ear.

BEWARE OF SORCERERS!

If you are still sick, your Aztec friends may take you to a sorcerer, or healer, known as a *tlacatecolotl*. Don't be surprised if he throws a bundle of rods on the ground. He will examine the pattern to figure out what's wrong with you. Then he may give you drugs made from cactus juice, which will give you very strange **hallucinations**.

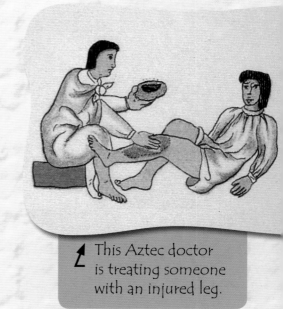

This Aztec doctor is treating someone with an injured leg.

STAYING SAFE

You will need to stay alert in the Aztec Empire. Stay away from priests with sacrificial knives, and watch out for warriors. Aztec knights are terrifying. They paint their faces and wear headdresses made from feathers. Aztecs fight with **javelins** and large two-handed swords. The swords have razor-sharp blades made from **flint**. In battle, the Aztecs sometimes use their swords to slice off their enemies' ears!

WILD WARRIORS

The wildest warriors are the jaguar and eagle knights. Jaguar knights dress in suits made from jaguar skins, with a snarling jaguar's head for their helmet. Eagle knights (like the one in this picture) wear suits of eagle feathers, complete with eagle's talons, head, and beak.

CRIME AND PUNISHMENT

Be sure to stay out of trouble during your visit. Aztec punishments are very harsh. If people are found drunk in the street, their heads are shaved and their houses are knocked down. If they fail to learn their lesson and get drunk again, they are killed instantly. You must also be very careful not to act above your class. Commoners who dare to wear perfume, buy presents of roses, or drink hot chocolate are punished by instant death.

RESPECT OR DEATH

If you happen to catch sight of the emperor, quickly turn away. No one is allowed to look at his face, touch him, or see him eat. People who dare to break these rules are instantly put to death.

This Aztec temple in Acatitlan, Mexico, was dedicated to the rain god and sun god.

CHAPTER 7

AZTEC EMPIRE FACTS AND FIGURES

Are you a little unsure about the main events and dates in Aztec history? Would you like to know the full story of the fall of the Aztec Empire? And do you know how **historians** and **archaeologists** have managed to piece together their picture of the Aztec world? This section contains useful background information to fully prepare you for your trip to the Aztec Empire. It also includes a brief pronunciation guide so you can make yourself understood in the land of the Aztecs.

HOW WE KNOW ABOUT THE AZTECS

Over the last five centuries, historians and archaeologists have managed to piece together a remarkable picture of life in the Aztec Empire. This picture is largely thanks to the records of Spanish soldiers and early visitors to the Aztec Empire, but also to codices created by the Aztecs. In Mexico archaeologists have dug up statues, carvings, and ornaments in the remains of Aztec buildings.

THE SPANISH ARRIVE

In 1517 Spanish soldiers known as **conquistadors** had begun to advance into Mexico. One of the expeditions was led by Hernán Cortés. In March 1519 Cortés landed at Tabasco in southeast Mexico with an army of 608 soldiers. As soon as Cortés learned about the gold and riches of Tenochtitlán, he was determined to conquer the Aztecs.

A SOLDIER OR A GOD?

In November 1519 Cortés and his army marched north toward the city of Tenochtitlán. But instead of being met by fierce warriors, they were greeted with gifts. The Aztecs believed that Cortés was their fair-skinned god Quetzalcoatl coming to attack them because they had made him angry. The Aztec emperor Moctezuma decided to try to please his god by offering gifts.

HERNAN CORTES (1485–1547)

Hernán Cortés was a Spanish soldier who was put in charge of an expedition to reach the Mexican mainland. He eventually became governor of Mexico, which he named New Spain. Cortés led several unsuccessful expeditions into other parts of America. He finally returned to Spain in 1540, where he died seven years later.

A CRUEL MOVE

Moctezuma decided to entertain Cortés in his city. But Cortés was impatient to gain control of the palace. He persuaded Moctezuma that he should move out and set up court in a separate building. Then, Cortés seized the royal palace for himself and surrounded Moctezuma's new headquarters with troops. Cortés gained control of the Aztec Empire, and the emperor became his prisoner.

EMPEROR MOCTEZUMA II (1480–1520)

Moctezuma II was the last Aztec emperor. At first he was a good military leader, and the empire reached its greatest size during his reign. However, Moctezuma was a vain and proud ruler who treated the common people harshly. He was killed in 1520 by his own people.

THE END OF THE EMPIRE

The following year a rival Spanish expedition tried to capture the lands won by Cortés. Cortés defeated them, but while he was away fighting, the people of Tenochtitlán rose in rebellion against their Spanish rulers. When Cortés returned, he found his soldiers and Emperor Moctezuma hiding from the angry citizens. He persuaded Moctezuma to address his people from a tower, but he was showered with weapons and later died from his wounds.

After this disaster, Cortés withdrew from Tenochtitlán. However, a year later, on August 13, 1521, he attacked the city again. This time the Aztecs did not resist, and the Spanish conquest of the Aztec Empire was complete.

AZTEC HISTORY AT A GLANCE

TIMELINE

(Note: dates given are approximate.)

9000 BCE	People begin to settle in the Valley of Mexico
1500 BCE	The Maya civilization has its origins in the Yucatan peninsula
250 CE	The Maya are building cities in many parts of Mexico
850	The Maya are driven out of most of their Mexican towns by neighboring tribes
950	The Toltecs build Tula and become the most powerful Mexican people
1100–1200	The Aztecs leave their homeland in northern Mexico and start to move south
1168	Tula is destroyed by rival Mexican tribes, and the Toltecs escape to the Yucatan peninsula
1300	The Aztecs arrive in the Valley of Mexico
1325	The Aztecs settle beside Lake Texcoco; they start to build the city of Tenochtitlán on islands in the lake
1376	Acamapichtli becomes the first *tlatoani* (emperor); the Aztecs are at war with many neighboring tribes
1428	The Aztecs and their allies conquer the Tepanec Empire and become the chief powers in the Valley of Mexico
1458	The Aztecs take over large areas of land around the Gulf of Mexico
1487	The Great Temple in Tenochtitlán is rebuilt, bigger than ever

1502	Moctezuma II becomes the last Aztec emperor
1504	Start of a three-year period of bad omens (famine, plagues, and earthquake)
1519	March 12: Hernán Cortés lands in southeast Mexico; on November 8 Cortés reached Tenochtitlán and takes Moctezuma II prisoner
1520	The Aztecs attack the Spaniards; Moctezuma dies
1521	On April 28 the Siege of Tenochtitlán begins; on August 13 the Spaniards take over the ruins of Tenochtitlán
1535	Mexico becomes a colony of Spain
1540s	Aztec scribes create a document known as the Codex Mendoza. It contains a picture record of the Aztecs' way of life.
1790	Workers in Mexico City discover a huge statue of the Aztec goddess Coatlicue
1791	Workers uncover the Aztec Stone of the Sun (see page 21)
1900	Aztec remains are found when sewers are laid in Mexico City
1978-1982	The remains of the Great Temple of Tenochtitlán are **excavated**
1989	An Aztec palace is found at Yautepec, south of Mexico city
2001	A shrine to the rain god Tlaloc is discovered on the Pico de Orizaba mountain, in Mexico

SPEAK LIKE THE AZTECS

The Aztec people speak Nahuatl (say "*nah-wah-tl*"), a language that is still spoken in Mexico today. Aztec words and names can seem difficult to pronounce when you see them written down, but there are a few basic rules to follow. If you stick to these guidelines, you should be able to pronounce even the most complicated names!

PRONUNCIATION GUIDE

X is pronounced like *SH* in "English".
TL sounds like the *TL* in "faintly" (but without the sound of the "y").
CU is pronounced *KW*.
HU is pronounced like *W* in "win".
Z is pronounced like *S* in "English".

SOME COMMON AZTEC WORDS

The Aztecs usually stress the second from last **syllable** in a word. (Stress the syllable in <u>underline</u>.)

Huitzilopochtli	*Weet-see-lo-<u>pocht</u>-lee*
Nahuatl (the Aztec language)	*Na-<u>wah</u>-tl*
Quetzalcoatl (the serpent god, god of creation)	*Ket-zal-<u>ko</u>-wat*
Tenochtitlán	*Te-noch-<u>teet</u>-lan*
Teotihuacán	*Tay-oh-tee-<u>wah</u>-kan*
Texcoco	*Tesh-<u>co</u>-co*
tlacatecolotl (sorcerer)	*tla-kat-ek-<u>ol</u>-otl*
tlachtli (sacred ball game)	*tlash-<u>tlee</u>*
Tlaloc (god of rain)	*Tla-<u>lok</u>*
tlamatini (doctor)	*tla-mat-<u>ee</u>-nee*
tlatoani (emperor)	*tla-to-<u>ah</u>-nee*
Moctezuma (last Aztec emperor)	*Mo-te-<u>zo</u>-ma*

FURTHER READING

BOOKS

Jovinelly, Joann *et al. The Crafts and Culture of the Aztecs.* New York: Rosen Publishing Group, 2002

Rees, Rosemary. *The Aztecs.* Chicago: Heinemann Library, 2001

Santella, Andrew. *The Aztec.* Minneapolis: Sagebrush Education Resources, 2003

Stout, Mary A. *Aztec.* Milwaukee, WI: Gareth Stevens Inc., 2003

WEBSITES

• http://www.pbs.org/conquistadors/cortes/cortes_a00.html

• http://www.latinamericanstudies.org/aztecs.htm

GLOSSARY

archaeologist someone who learns about the past by digging up old buildings and objects and examining them

barter to trade by exchanging goods, rather than paying for goods with money

cacao beans beans used to produce chocolate

causeway raised road that connects an island to the mainland

ceremonial used for religious ceremonies, services, and festivals

city-state city that has its own rulers and laws

codex type of early book, often made from a long strip of folded paper

commoner member of the ordinary people, not a noble or a priest

conquistador soldier who conquers land and people in a foreign land

cultivated farmed land with crops

drought long period of very dry weather

excavated dug up

famine serious shortage of food

fast period of not eating food for religious reasons

fertile good for growing plants and crops

flint very hard stone that is good for building and making tools

glyph picture that is used to represent an object

hallucination strange sights that you believe you are seeing, but do not really exist

historian someone who studies events and people from the past

incense substance that is burned to create a sweet smell

inlaid set into the surface of something

javelin long-handled spear

locust insect similar to a grasshopper that destroys crops

mainland main part of a country, not an island

mason someone who cuts and carves stone and builds stone buildings

merchant someone who trades goods, often traveling long distances with goods to trade

mineral substance found in the earth, such as iron, salt, or diamonds

observatory building used for studying the stars

plague serious disease that spreads very fast

prescribe to tell a patient what medicine to take

quarry to dig for rocks or minerals

quill long, hollow central part of a bird's feather

remedy cure for an illness

reservoir large lake, used for storing water

sacrifice animal or a human that is killed as a gift for the gods

shrine small temple built in honor of a god

smallpox serious disease that causes people to have a very high temperature and to be covered in red spots

splint piece of wood, used to support a broken or damaged arm or leg

story floor of a building

syllable one of the sounds in a word

terraced cut out of a hillside like steps

tribute gifts that conquered people have to give to their conquerors, as a form of tax

weave to make cloth by passing threads over and under each other

INDEX

bartering 45, 47
bathhouses 16

cactus 15, 18, 22, 52
calendars 20–21, 40
canoes 34
chilis 36, 37
chocolate 37
city-states 8
clans 14
clothes 15–17
codex/codices 20, 56
conquered tribes 8, 15
Cortés, Hernán 9, 27, 56, 57, 59
councils 14
crafts 12, 14, 18, 48–49
crime and punishment 53

doctors 52
drought 11

education 19
emperors 8, 13, 14, 15, 30, 35, 37, 38, 53

farming 8, 9, 11–12, 14, 18
featherwork 17, 30, 49, 53
festivals 20, 40, 49
fishing 34

glyphs 20
gods and goddesses 11, 12, 22–23, 27, 28, 29, 40, 54, 56
gold 12, 15, 17, 29, 47, 48, 56

health and medicine 51, 52

houses 34, 35
Huitzilopochtli 22, 23, 27, 28, 29
human sacrifices 11, 13, 15, 22, 29, 31, 35, 40, 41, 43, 50
hunting 37

jewelry 15, 17, 48

knights 15, 41, 53

Lake Texcoco 8, 12, 26, 34, 58
language 60
legends 26, 29

markets 27, 44, 45, 46–49
marriage 19, 40
masks 14, 23, 29, 48
Maya 31, 43, 58
Mexico City 27
mineral resources 12
Moctezuma II 13, 27, 30, 56–57, 59
mountains 11, 16

New Fire ceremony 21, 40–41
nobles 13, 14, 15, 17, 18, 19, 35, 49

obsidian 12, 48

palaces 30–31, 42
picture writing 20, 26
pottery 49
priests 15, 19, 20, 22, 30, 49, 53

prisoners 15, 22, 23, 31, 41, 43
pyramids 27, 28, 42

quetzal bird 23, 30
Quetzalcoatl 23, 56

rainforests 6, 10, 11, 39
religion 22–23

sacred ball game 31
serpent woman 14
slaves 13, 31, 34
smallpox 9
sorcerers 52
Spanish invaders 8, 9, 27, 56–57, 59

temples 19, 22, 23, 27, 28, 29, 42, 54
Tenochtitlán 7, 8, 23, 24–31, 34, 40, 41, 44, 46, 57, 58, 59
Teotihuacán 42
Tlateloco 27, 46
Toltecs 43, 58
tortillas 36
trade 8, 47
tribute 15
Tula 43, 58

volcanoes 12

War of Flowers 41
weapons 12, 48, 50, 53
weddings 40

zoo 30